D1607174

Llamas

ABDO
Publishing Company

A Buddy Book
by
Julie Murray

VISIT US AT
www.abdopub.com

Published by Buddy Books, an imprint of ABDO Publishing Company, 4940 Viking Drive, Suite 622, Edina, Minnesota 55435. Copyright © 2003 by Abdo Consulting Group, Inc. International copyrights reserved in all countries. No part of this book may be reproduced in any form without written permission from the publisher.

Printed in the United States.

Edited by: Christy DeVillier
Contributing Editors: Matt Ray, Michael P. Goecke
Graphic Design: Maria Hosley
Image Research: Deborah Coldiron
Photographs: Bill Campbell, M.D., Digital Stock, Geoatlas, Eyewire Inc., Photodisc

Library of Congress Cataloging-in-Publication Data

Murray, Julie, 1969-
  Llamas/Julie Murray.
      p. cm. — (Animal kingdom)
  Summary: An introduction to the physical characteristics, behavior, habitat, and life cycle of llamas, animals that originated in the western part of South America and are related to camels.
  ISBN 1-57765-724-1
    1. Llamas—Juvenile literature. [1. Llamas.] I. Title.

QL737 .U54 M87 2002
599.63'67—dc21

2001058960

Contents

Llamas

South Americans have been keeping llamas for more than 4,000 years. They used llama **fleece** to make rugs and clothes. Llama **dung** helped their fires burn.

South Americans used llamas as **pack animals**, too. Pack animals carry things for people.

Llamas have been living in South America for thousands of years.

What They Are Like

Llamas are gentle and calm. They like to be with each other. Llamas get along with sheep, goats, and horses. They are good with children, too. Some people keep llamas as pets.

Llamas will spit if they are scared or angry. Llamas mostly spit at other llamas. They do not commonly spit at people.

Llamas are gentle animals.

Llama Sounds

Llamas are mostly quiet. But they will call out if they see danger. Llamas also cluck, snort, and hum. They may hum when they are hot or upset. Mother llamas hum to their babies, too.

What They Look Like

Llamas look a lot like camels. They have camel-like faces with big eyes. Like camels, llamas have two toes on each foot. And llamas hold their long necks upright, like camels.

Llamas are smaller than camels.
Llamas grow to become five to six feet
(two m) tall.

Camel

Llama

Camels are relatives of llamas.

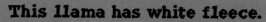
This llama has white fleece.

Llamas have a thick coat of hair called **fleece**. A llama's fleece may be white, brown, or black. Some llamas are only one color. Llamas can have a mixed coat of colors, too.

Where They Live

At one time, wild llamas lived in the Andes Mountains. These mountains are on South America's west coast. Wild llamas lived together in groups, or herds. Today, people in many places have llamas.

Wild llamas lived in the Andes
Mountains of South America.

Llamas As Guards

Some llamas live on sheep and goat farms. Llamas are good for guarding sheep and goats. They

keep these animals safe from **predators**. These llamas watch out for wolves and coyotes.

Eating

Llamas are plant-eaters. They use their lips and lower teeth to grab leaves. They chew food with their back teeth. Llamas eat leaves, weeds, grass, and hay.

Llamas eat grass and weeds.

Llamas have a three-part stomach. After swallowing, food goes down to one part of the llama's stomach. Later, this food comes back up to the llama's mouth. The llama will chew this food, or **cud**, and swallow again. Cows and sheep chew their cud, too.

Llamas have a three-part stomach.

Llama Crias

Female llamas have one baby at a time. A baby llama is called a cria. Newborn crias weigh about 25 pounds (11 kg) each. They can stand up very soon after birth.

A baby llama is called a cria.

Young llamas drink their mother's milk for about six months. They are adults by the age of two or three. Llamas can live for 25 years.

Llamas Today

Some people raise llamas for their **fleece**. Llama fleece is good for making hats, scarves, or blankets.

Some people keep llamas for their fleece.

Hikers sometimes use llamas as pack animals.

Some people take llamas with them on mountain hikes. They help hikers carry their things. Llamas can carry as much as 100 pounds (45 kg).

Important Words

cud swallowed food from the stomach of a llama. Cows and sheep also chew their cud.

dung an animal's solid waste.

fleece a llama's coat of hair.

pack animal an animal that carries things for people.

predator an animal that hunts and eats other animals.

Web Sites

LlamaWeb

www.llamaweb.com
Read more about llamas and their relatives.

Charismatic Llamas

www.eskimo.com/~wallama/faq.htm
This site features questions and answers about llamas.

Cappy's Place

www.shagbarkridge.com/cappy.html
This site is "hosted" by Cappy the Llama. It has games, letters to Cappy, and pictures of his llama friends.

Index